My United States

Illinois

WITHDRAWN

JOSH GREGORY

Children's Press®
An Imprint of Scholastic Inc.

Content Consultant

James Wolfinger, PhD, Associate Dean and Professor
College of Education, DePaul University, Chicago, Illinois

Library of Congress Cataloging-in-Publication Data
Names: Gregory, Josh, author.
Title: Illinois / by Josh Gregory.
Description: New York, NY : Children's Press, an imprint of Scholastic Inc., [2017] | Series: A true book | Includes bibliographical references and index.
Identifiers: LCCN 2016056324| ISBN 9780531252567 (library binding : alk. paper) | ISBN 9780531232866 (pbk. : alk. paper)
Subjects: LCSH: Illinois—Juvenile literature.
Classification: LCC F541.3 .G74 2017 | DDC 977.3—dc23
LC record available at https://lccn.loc.gov/2016056324

Photographs ©: cover: Evgeny Moerman/Dreamstime; back cover ribbon: AliceLiddelle/Getty Images; back cover bottom: Maks Narodenko/Shutterstock; 3 bottom: Wiskerke/Alamy Images; 3 map: Jim McMahon; 4 bottom: Dan Thornberg/Shutterstock; 4 top: Stock Connection/Superstock, Inc.; 5 bottom: outtakes/iStockphoto; 5 top: John J. Kim/TNS/Newscom; 6 center bottom: Pamela Brick/Shutterstock; 6 top: Chuck Eckert/Getty Images; 6 bottom: Don Smetzer/Alamy Images; 6 center top: FeyginFoto/Shutterstock; 8-9: marchello74/iStockphoto; 11: snikeltrut/iStockphoto; 12: Jim Reed/Media Bakery; 13: dmodlino1/iStockphoto; 14: FrankHildebrand/iStockphoto; 15: Brian J. Skerry/Getty Images; 16-17: DenisTangneyJr/iStockphoto; 19: Seth Perlman/AP Images; 20: Tigatelu/iStockphoto; 22 right: Pakmor/Shutterstock; 22 left: Alan Cotton/Alamy Images; 23 center right: xfotostudio/iStockphoto; 23 top left: Gail Jankus/Science Source; 23 bottom right: outtakes/iStockphoto; 23 top right: Stock Connection/Superstock, Inc.; 23 bottom left: Dan Thornberg/Shutterstock; 23 center left: gsagi/iStockphoto; 24-25: Jonathan Blair/Getty Images; 27: North Wind Picture Archives/Alamy Images; 29: Science Source; 30: Don Smetzer/Alamy Images; 31 right: North Wind Picture Archives/Alamy Images; 31 left: Alan Cotton/Alamy Images; 32: Bloomberg/Getty Images; 33: Pictorial Press Ltd/Alamy Images; 34-35 background: f11photo/Shutterstock; 35 inset: Michael Weber/Media Bakery; 36: John J. Kim/TNS/Newscom; 37: Russell Gordon/DanitaDelimont.com "Danita Delimont Photography"/Newscom; 38: Lya_Cattel/iStockphoto; 39: Maskot/Superstock, Inc.; 40 inset: prairie_eye/iStockphoto; 40 bottom: PepitoPhotos/iStockphoto; 41: Helen Sessions/age fotostock; 42 top left: The Granger Collection; 42 top right: Pictorial Press Ltd/Alamy Images; 42 center left: Nordic Photos/Superstock, Inc.; 42 center right: Pictorial Press Ltd/Alamy Images; 42 bottom: CSU Archives/Everett Collection; 43 top left: Paramount Pictures/Everett Collection; 43 center left: Tannen Maury/epa european pressphoto agency b.v./Alamy Images; 43 top right: Crush Rush/Shutterstock; 43 bottom left: Riccardo De Luca/ZUMA Press/Newscom; 43 bottom center: Parisa/Newscom; 43 center right: Amanda Lucidon/ZUMA Press/Newscom; 43 bottom right: Kamil KrzaczynskiEPA/Newscom; 44 bottom: Chicago History Museum/Getty Images; 44 top: snikeltrut/iStockphoto; 45 center: George Dolgikh/Shutterstock; 45 top: North Wind Picture Archives/Alamy Images; 45 bottom: gsagi/iStockphoto.

Maps by Map Hero, Inc.

SCHOLASTIC, CHILDREN'S PRESS, A TRUE BOOK™, and associated logos are trademarks and/or registered trademarks of Scholastic Inc., 557 Broadway, New York, NY 10012.
1 2 3 4 5 6 7 8 9 10 R 27 26 25 24 23 22 21 20 19 18

Front cover: Chicago skyline
Back cover: Ears of corn

Welcome to Illinois

Illinois →

Find the Truth!

Everything you are about to read is true **except** for one of the sentences on this page.

Which one is **TRUE**?

T or F Illinois's state animal is the white-tailed deer.

T or F Illinois was one of the original 13 states.

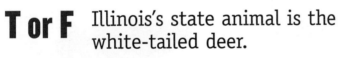

Find the answers in this book.

3

Contents

THE BIG TRUTH!

Monarch
butterfly

What Represents Illinois?

Bluegill

Chicago Cubs fans

3 History

How did Illinois become
the state it is today? 25

4 Culture

What do Illinoisans do for work and fun? 35

Cardinal

5

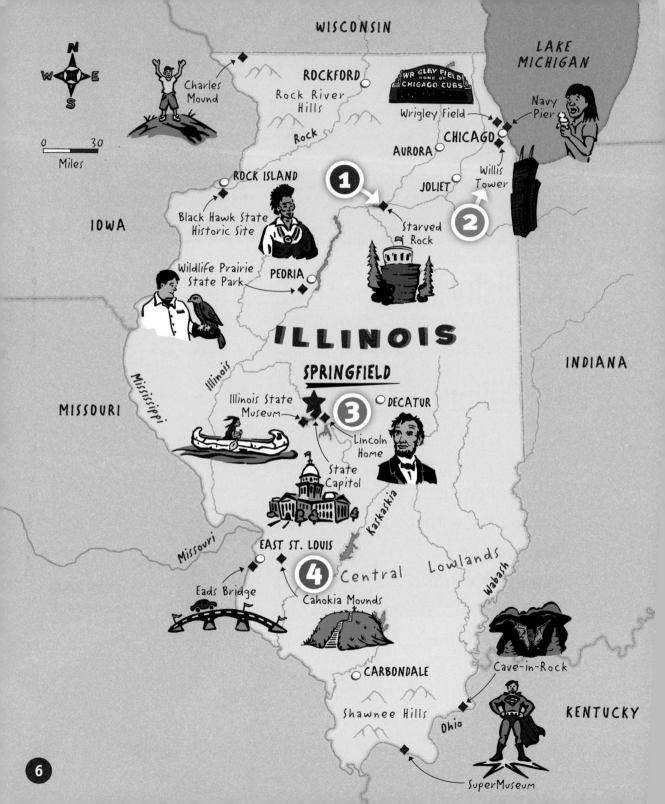

WISCONSIN

LAKE MICHIGAN

N W E S

Charles Mound

ROCKFORD
Rock River Hills

Rock

WR GLEY FIELD HOME OF CHICAGO CUBS

Wrigley Field

Navy Pier

CHICAGO

AURORA

JOLIET

Willis Tower

1

2

Starved Rock

ROCK ISLAND

IOWA

Black Hawk State Historic Site

Wildlife Prairie State Park

PEORIA

ILLINOIS

INDIANA

SPRINGFIELD

Illinois

Mississippi

MISSOURI

Illinois State Museum

DECATUR

3

Lincoln Home

State Capitol

Kaskaskia

Missouri

EAST ST. LOUIS

4

Central

Lowlands

Wabash

Eads Bridge

Cahokia Mounds

Cave-in-Rock

CARBONDALE

Shawnee Hills

Ohio

KENTUCKY

SuperMuseum

0   30
Miles

This Is Illinois!

① Starved Rock State Park

This beautiful park is famous for its steep canyons, woods, and waterfalls. Visit to enjoy hiking, camping, and more!

② Willis Tower

This skyscraper is the tallest building in Illinois and the second-tallest in the United States. Visitors can take in the view from the Skydeck Ledge, a glass box that extends out from the building's 103rd floor.

③ Lincoln Home

The house where Abraham Lincoln lived in Springfield has been preserved as a national historic site. Take a tour to get a glimpse into the life of one of the country's greatest presidents.

④ Cahokia Mounds

Hundreds of years ago, the Mississippian people established Cahokia, a city that became home to thousands of residents. There, they built more than 100 enormous mounds out of earth.

Chicago is home to more than 2.7 million people.

CHAPTER 1

Land and Wildlife

Illinois is a land of contrasts. Three-quarters of the state's population lives crowded in the urban areas surrounding Chicago, the nation's third-largest city. Everywhere else, vast fields of corn, beans, and other crops stretch for miles in all directions. Let's take a closer look at this beautiful state.

The Lay of the Land

Illinois is not a land of mountain peaks or deep valleys. From one end to the other, it is mostly flat. The only exceptions are the far southern and northwestern parts of the state, where you'll find beautiful green hills. The northeast is occupied by the city of Chicago and its many **suburbs**. Here, you'll also find the shores of Lake Michigan. Along the state's western border lies the Mississippi River, its other major body of water.

This map shows where Illinois's higher (yellow and orange) and lower (light and dark green) areas are.

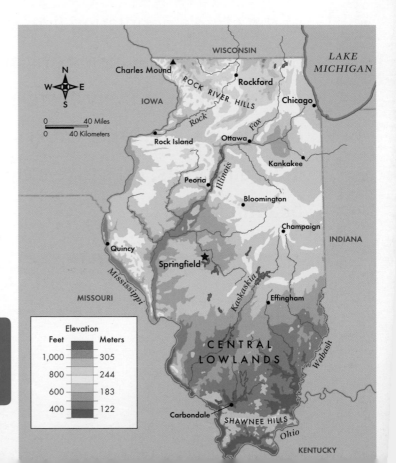

The Mighty Mississippi

The Mississippi is the chief river in North America. It begins in Minnesota and flows all the way to the Gulf of Mexico. Because of its length and convenient location in the center of the country, it has long played an important role in the U.S. economy. Illinois businesses have relied on the river to exchange goods with other states and even internationally. As a result, many towns are located along its banks.

Wild Weather

Illinois experiences a wide range of weather, with drastic changes in temperature and **precipitation** from season to season. The state has seen temperatures as high as 117 degrees Fahrenheit (47 degrees Celsius) in the summer and as low as −36°F (−38°C) in the winter. On average, it is slightly warmer and rainier in the southern parts of the state, while the north is cooler and receives less precipitation. Thunderstorms and tornadoes are common across the state, so watch out!

On average, Illinois sees more than 60 tornadoes per year.

MAXIMUM TEMPERATURE
117°F

MINIMUM TEMPERATURE
−36°F

More than 250 kinds of trees grow in Illinois, including those along the sandy beaches of Lake Michigan.

Plant Life

Forests and **prairies** make up most of the natural landscapes in Illinois. In the state's forests, you'll find a wide variety of trees, including oak, maple, walnut, pine, and hickory. In the prairies, you'll brush up against a number of tall grasses. You'll also see brightly colored wildflowers such as sunflowers and violets. Altogether, about 2,500 plant species are **native** to Illinois.

Animals

As you explore the outdoors in Illinois, you'll see a huge variety of animal species. Many of these wild animals can be found not only in natural areas but also in towns and cities. White-tailed deer, squirrels, coyotes, and rabbits are all common. Birds such as blue jays, cardinals, and robins are easy to spot flying above. Large birds such as turkeys, owls, and eagles also live in Illinois.

Cliff-dwelling peregrine falcons feel at home among Chicago's skyscrapers.

The state's rivers and lakes are home to many animal species. If you go fishing, you might catch bluegills, bass, walleye, or catfish. You might also see frogs or salamanders near the shallow edges of the water. Snakes and turtles are a common sight in many areas, too.

Illinois has had four different constitutions since becoming a state.

CHAPTER 2

Government

Since 1839, the city of Springfield has served as the capital of Illinois. It is here that the state's leaders gather to carry out the law of the land.

Illinois adopted its current constitution in 1970. This document outlines how the state's government should be organized and how elections work in Illinois. It also contains other guidelines for the way different parts of the government should operate.

State Government Basics

Like the U.S. government, the Illinois government is divided into three branches: the executive, the legislative, and the judicial. Led by the governor, the executive branch carries out the state's laws. Illinois's legislative branch is called the General Assembly. The General Assembly makes new laws. It is made up of a 59-member Senate and a 118-member House of Representatives.

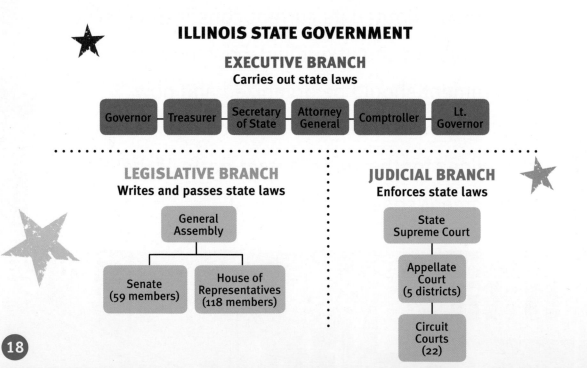

ILLINOIS STATE GOVERNMENT

EXECUTIVE BRANCH
Carries out state laws

Governor — Treasurer — Secretary of State — Attorney General — Comptroller — Lt. Governor

LEGISLATIVE BRANCH
Writes and passes state laws

General Assembly

Senate (59 members)

House of Representatives (118 members)

JUDICIAL BRANCH
Enforces state laws

State Supreme Court

Appellate Court (5 districts)

Circuit Courts (22)

Illinois's Legal System

Illinois's judicial branch consists of three court systems. Circuit courts hear cases when people are accused of breaking the law. Those who are found guilty in a circuit court case can **appeal** the court's decision. The case then goes before the state's appellate court. If someone appeals an appellate court decision, the case can reach the Illinois Supreme Court. The Supreme Court is made up of seven judges called justices. Their decision is the final word in all Illinois court cases.

Illinois in the National Government

Each state elects officials to represent it in the U.S. Congress. Like every state, Illinois has two senators. The U.S. House of Representatives relies on a state's population to determine its numbers. With a fairly large population, Illinois has 18 representatives in the House.

Each state also has a certain number of votes to apply in the election of the U.S. president. These electoral votes are equal to the number of members of Congress. With 2 senators and 18 representatives, Illinois has 20 electoral votes.

2 senators and 18 representatives

20 electoral votes

With 20 electoral votes, Illinois has a strong voice in presidential elections.

Representing Illinois

Elected officials in Illinois represent a population with a range of interests, lifestyles, and backgrounds.

Ethnicity (2015 estimates)

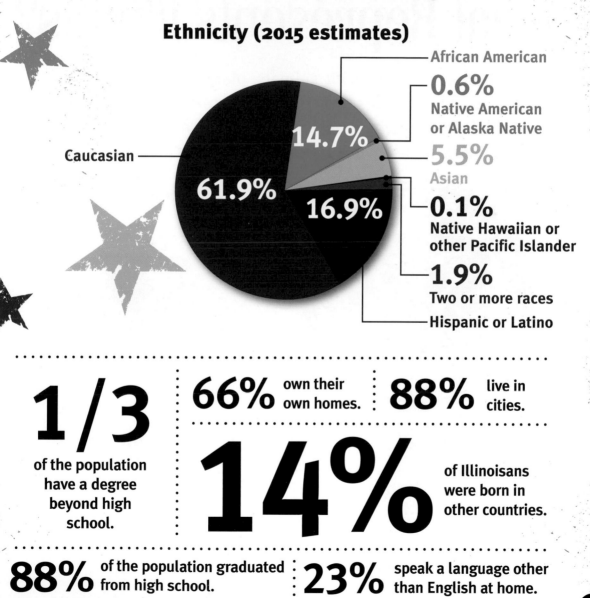

African American
14.7%

0.6%
Native American or Alaska Native

5.5%
Asian

0.1%
Native Hawaiian or other Pacific Islander

1.9%
Two or more races

Caucasian
61.9%

16.9%
Hispanic or Latino

1/3 of the population have a degree beyond high school.

66% own their own homes.

88% live in cities.

14% of Illinoisans were born in other countries.

88% of the population graduated from high school.

23% speak a language other than English at home.

What Represents Illinois?

States choose specific animals, plants, and objects to represent the values and characteristics of the land and its people. Find out why these symbols were chosen to represent Illinois or discover surprising curiosities about them.

Seal

Illinois's current state seal was adopted in 1867. It is based on a design created in 1819, soon after Illinois became a state. The banner in the eagle's beak reads "State **Sovereignty**, National Union," which is the Illinois state motto.

Flag

Adopted in 1915, the state flag displays the same artwork as the state seal on a white background. In 1970, the state's name was added below the seal.

Violet

STATE FLOWER

These beautiful purple flowers bloom all across Illinois each spring.

Monarch Butterfly

STATE INSECT

These brightly colored butterflies can be found in Illinois each year between May and October.

Popcorn

STATE SNACK FOOD

Illinois farmers grow a lot of corn, so it's no surprise that popcorn is the official state snack!

White-tailed Deer

STATE ANIMAL

You can see these deer almost anywhere you go in Illinois, from forests to towns.

Bluegill

STATE FISH

Illinois fishers love catching these small fish in the state's many lakes.

Cardinal

STATE BIRD

This bright red bird was chosen to represent Illinois by schoolchildren in 1928.

CHAPTER 3

History

People first came to the area that would become Illinois sometime between 20,000 and 8000 BCE. These prehistoric people came to southern Illinois in pursuit of **mammoths** and other animals. The people lived in caves and moved around often. But by about 2000 BCE, many of the animals they relied on for food had died out. The people began to build permanent homes and rely more on plant foods.

Illinois's First City

Around 850 CE, a group of people called the Mississippians moved into what is now southern Illinois. They lived in a settlement called Cahokia. There they raised many crops. They also shaped huge, impressive mounds out of dirt. Cahokia grew quickly. By 1150 it was home to about 20,000 people. However, for unknown reasons, the Mississippians eventually began to leave. By about 1400, Cahokia was abandoned.

This map shows the general areas where Native American groups settled before Europeans arrived.

Many Native Americans in Illinois lived in wigwams, which were wooden frames covered with animal skins, grass, or other materials.

New Residents

Beginning in the 1500s, other groups of Native Americans began moving into Illinois. While each of these groups had its own culture and leaders, they all spoke a group of related languages called Algonquian. They got along well and cooperated with each other, and their culture flourished. By 1650, there were around 16,500 Algonquian-speaking people living in Illinois.

The French Arrive

In 1673, French explorers Louis Jolliet and Jacques Marquette set sail across Lake Michigan from Canada. Traveling southwest, they eventually reached Illinois, becoming the first Europeans to visit the area. They soon met a group of people who introduced themselves as *Illiniwek*, an Algonquian word meaning "men." The French explorers wrote the word as "Illinois."

This map shows the routes taken by French explorers in the 1600s.

George Washington (on horseback) leads British forces during the French and Indian War.

The French and Indian War

The French and the Algonquian-speaking peoples got along well. However, other Europeans were also staking their claim on land in North America. They began to fight among themselves for control of the continent. In 1756, war broke out between Great Britain and France. Fighting on France's side were its Native American allies. After seven long years of fighting, Great Britain won the war. As a result, it took control of all land east of the Mississippi River, including Illinois.

The 21st State

Around the same time, tension was building between British **colonists** and the government of Great Britain. The colonists wanted to govern themselves. Between 1775 and 1783, they fought and won the American Revolution. As a result, the 13 colonies along the East Coast became the United States. Over time, people began moving westward and settling in Illinois and other areas.

Timeline of Illinois Events

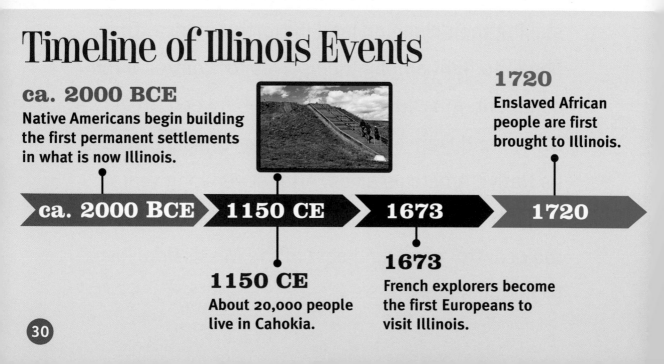

ca. 2000 BCE
Native Americans begin building the first permanent settlements in what is now Illinois.

1720
Enslaved African people are first brought to Illinois.

ca. 2000 BCE — 1150 CE — 1673 — 1720

1150 CE
About 20,000 people live in Cahokia.

1673
French explorers become the first Europeans to visit Illinois.

Modern History

On December 3, 1818, Illinois became the 21st state. In the following decades, Illinois's population exploded. Many eastern settlers moved westward to make their home in the new state. Many **immigrants** also came from Europe, especially Germany and Ireland. These people set up farms, towns, and cities in their new home. By 1900, Illinois was home to almost five million people.

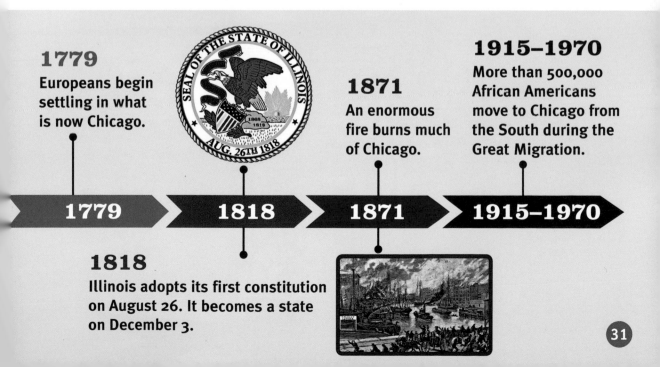

1779
Europeans begin settling in what is now Chicago.

1871
An enormous fire burns much of Chicago.

1915–1970
More than 500,000 African Americans move to Chicago from the South during the Great Migration.

| 1779 | 1818 | 1871 | 1915–1970 |

1818
Illinois adopts its first constitution on August 26. It becomes a state on December 3.

Illinois's location, excellent transportation, and wealth of natural resources soon made it one of the nation's main economic centers. Chicago became known for its meatpacking and manufacturing industries. In the 20th century, the jobs provided by these and other industries drew immigrants from all over the world. As a result, the state is now home to a diverse range of people.

A worker assembles coffee grinding equipment at a Chicago factory.

Abraham Lincoln, the 16th President

Abraham Lincoln is one of the most famous Illinoisans in history. Lincoln moved to Illinois in 1830, at the age of 21. Four years later, he was elected a state representative. He also became a successful lawyer. In 1858, he ran for one of Illinois's seats in the U.S. Senate. He lost, but his inspiring debate performances during the campaign made him famous. In 1860, he ran for president and won. As president, he led the country through the Civil War (1861–1865) and helped end slavery. Sadly, he was assassinated just as the war was ending. Today, Illinois is nicknamed Land of Lincoln in his honor.

Daniel Day-Lewis in *Lincoln* (2012)

CHAPTER 4

Culture

There is no lack of things to do in Illinois. Chicago is Illinois's cultural hub. The city is noted for its great restaurants, excellent museums, and countless other attractions. But there is more to Illinois than just its largest city. Outside Chicago, the rest of the state offers plenty to do and see.

A sightseeing tour bus in Chicago

Fans celebrate the Chicago Cubs' World Series victory in 2016.

The Old Ball Game

Many pro sports teams play in Chicago and the surrounding area. Basketball fans follow the Chicago Bulls, while football fans pack Soldier Field to watch the Chicago Bears in action. In hockey, the Chicago Blackhawks have won three Stanley Cup championships since 2010. Two Major League Baseball teams play in Chicago: the White Sox and the Cubs. In 2016, the Cubs won the World Series for the first time in 108 years!

Illinois Celebrations

People in Illinois love to have a good time. Every August, people from all over the state gather in Springfield for the Illinois State Fair. They enjoy food and entertainment, and the state's farmers show off their most impressive livestock. In early July, huge crowds head to Chicago for the world's largest food festival. At this event, called the Taste of Chicago, attendees can sample an enormous variety of delicious foods.

People celebrate the Moon Festival in Chicago's Chinatown neighborhood each autumn.

A film crew works at a movie set in downtown Chicago. The city's film industry is growing rapidly.

Illinois Industries

Illinois's thriving economy is built around a wide variety of businesses. With farmland covering 80 percent of the state, agriculture remains big business. Illinois manufacturers produce everything from tractors and cars to medicine and household goods. Chicago alone is home to hundreds of major corporations. People there work in just about every field imaginable, from banking and insurance to film and television production.

Changing Technology, Changing Jobs

Illinois has long been on the cutting edge of new and changing industries. For example, Illinois's biotechnology companies investigate ways of improving crops and medicine through science. And Chicago is one of the country's hot spots for tech jobs, with plenty of new companies forming every year to build tomorrow's top computer software and hardware.

39

A Bite to Eat

Illinois is home to just about every type of restaurant you can imagine. You'll have no trouble finding classic American dishes, ethnic favorites, or the latest culinary creations. Local specialties include deep-dish pizza, Italian beef sandwiches, and Chicago-style hot dogs.

★ Chicago-Style Hot Dogs

Hot dogs are a popular fast food in Illinois. Make sure you get the right combination of ingredients for the authentic Chicago flavor!

Ingredients

All-beef hot dogs
Hot dog buns with poppy seeds
Yellow mustard
Sweet pickle relish
Chopped white onion

Tomato sliced into thin wedges
Dill pickle spears
Sport peppers
Celery salt

Directions

Place the hot dogs in a pot of boiling water and cook until they are hot, about 5 minutes. Drain. Place each hot dog in a bun. Add plenty of mustard, relish, and onion. Now top each hot dog with one or two tomato wedges, a pickle spear, and two sport peppers. Finish them off with a sprinkle of celery salt and enjoy!

Cloud Gate, a sculpture in Chicago's Millennium Park, was inspired by the appearance of liquid mercury.

A Diverse State

From densely packed city streets to wide-open fields, Illinois is a land of great variety. In the Land of Lincoln live people from all around the world, speaking countless languages and working in a wide range of jobs. Some live in high-rise apartment houses, others on farms where the nearest neighbors are miles away. For residents and visitors alike, Illinois offers countless places and activities to enjoy. ★

Famous People

Jane Addams

(1860–1935) was an activist, writer, and social worker. In 1931, she became the first American woman to win the Nobel Peace Prize. Addams was born in Illinois and lived there most of her life.

Ida B. Wells

(1862–1931) was a journalist, civil rights leader, and founding member of the National Association for the Advancement of Colored People (NAACP). She lived in Illinois for much of her life.

Miles Davis

(1926–1991) was a trumpeter and composer. He is considered one of the greatest jazz musicians in history. Davis was born in Alton and grew up in East St. Louis.

Ernest Hemingway

(1899–1961) was a journalist and fiction author who wrote many books that are widely considered to be classics. He grew up in Oak Park.

Shel Silverstein

(1932–1999) was a poet, illustrator, musician, and playwright who is best known for books such as *The Giving Tree* and *Where the Sidewalk Ends*. He grew up in Chicago.

Harrison Ford

(1942–) is an actor who is famous for his roles in the *Star Wars* and *Indiana Jones* series and countless other films. He was born in Chicago.

Hillary Clinton

(1947–) is a former First Lady of the United States, U.S. senator, U.S. secretary of state, and presidential candidate. She grew up in Park Ridge.

Carol Moseley Braun

(1947–) is a lawyer and politician who was the first African American woman ever elected to the U.S. Senate. She was born and raised in Illinois and spent many years in state and local government there.

Sandra Cisneros

(1954–) is a writer who is best known for her 1984 novel *The House on Mango Street*. The book is based on her experiences growing up in Chicago. She grew up in Castle Rock.

Oprah Winfrey ★

(1954–) is a TV personality, actress, and businessperson who is best known for her long-running talk show, *The Oprah Winfrey Show*. The show was filmed in Chicago.

Michelle Obama

(1964–) is a lawyer, writer, and former First Lady of the United States. She was born and raised in Chicago.

Kanye West

(1977–) is a rapper, songwriter, record producer, and fashion designer who has won 21 Grammy Awards and is one of the best-selling artists of all time. He grew up in Chicago.

Did You Know That...

Illinois's highest point is at Charles Mound in northwestern Illinois, where the ground is 1,235 feet (376 meters) above sea level. Its lowest point is at the Mississippi River, measuring 279 feet (85 m) above sea level.

Illinois 1/12 the size of Alaska.

Illinois covers a total of 57,914 square miles (149,997 square kilometers).

The first skyscraper ever, the Home Insurance Building, was built in Chicago in 1885.

In 1871, a giant fire spread across Chicago, burning down more than 17,000 buildings.

Illinois farmers grow more pumpkins than any other state: 317.9 million pounds (144.2 million kilograms) in 2015!

Did you find the truth?

T Illinois's state animal is the white-tailed deer.

F Illinois was one of the original 13 states.

Resources

Books

Nonfiction

Benoit, Peter. *Abraham Lincoln*. New York: Children's Press, 2012.

Burgan, Michael. *Illinois*. New York: Children's Press, 2014.

Taylor-Butler, Christine. *Michelle Obama*. New York: Children's Press, 2015.

Fiction

Cisneros, Sandra. *The House on Mango Street*. Houston: Arte Publico Press, 1983.

Roth, Veronica. *Divergent*. New York: Katherine Tegen Books, 2011.

Movies

Chicago (2002)

Divergent (2014)

Ferris Bueller's Day Off (1986)

Home Alone (1990)

Mean Girls (2004)

National Lampoon's Christmas Vacation (1989)

Sixteen Candles (1994)

Wayne's World (1992)

White Heat (1949)

Visit this Scholastic website for more information on Illinois:

★ www.factsfornow.scholastic.com
Enter the keyword **Illinois**

Important Words

appeal (uh-PEEL) to apply to a higher court for a change to a legal decision

colonists (KAH-luh-nists) people who live in a colony or who help establish one

immigrants (IM-uh-gruhntz) people who move from one country to another and settle there

mammoths (MAM-uhthz) animals that looked like large elephants, with long, curved tusks and shaggy hair

native (NAY-tiv) describing an animal or plant that lives or grows naturally in a certain place

prairies (PRAIR-eez) large areas of flat or rolling grassland with few or no trees

precipitation (pri-sip-uh-TAY-shuhn) the falling of water from the sky in the form of rain, snow, hail, or sleet

sovereignty (SAHV-rin-tee) supreme authority or the power to rule

suburbs (SUHB-urbz) areas or districts close to the outer edge of a city

Index

Page numbers in **bold** indicate illustrations.

About the Author

Josh Gregory is the author of more than 100 books for kids. He has written about everything from animals to technology to history. A graduate of the University of Missouri–Columbia, he currently lives in Portland, Oregon.